Contents

Our sheet music includes fingering positions, letter-coded notation, and song lyrics for a 6-hole ocarina. Although your ocarina has just 6 holes, this small instrument can produce 10 natural notes, the full range from C to C, plus D and E of the next octave and 7 flat and sharp notes: a total of 17 notes.

C-major scale for 6-holes Ocarina

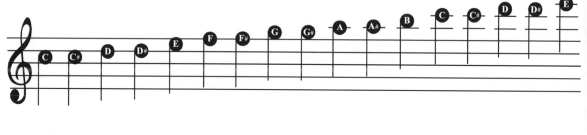

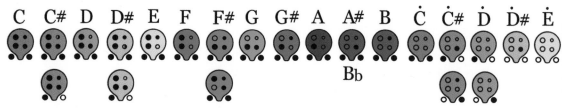

The fingering positions are shown in the book graphically on an image of a standard shaped ocarina with six holes. Each hole on the ocarina is represented by circles. The circles outside of the ocarina image represent the holes on the back side of the instrument. The circles filled in black indicate which holes should be covered while playing. The open circles mean they should be uncovered. The bottom circles correspond to the holes on the ocarina that are closest to your mouth. Circles on the left are played using the left hand and are played with the index and middle fingers, while those on the right side are played with the same fingers on the right hand.

As for the circles outside of the image, they indicate that your thumbs should be used on the holes underneath the instrument.

Ocarinas always have one hole which is never covered. This is the place where sound is released from the ocarina, which is called the whistle.

We present the fingering positions aimed at a C major 6-hole ocarina, which is the most popular model on the market. However, you can have E, F, G, B, and B-flat major ocarinas, which have different fingerings.

The 6-hole ocarina is an excellent beginner instrument. It is cheap (a well-tuned and perfect-sounding instrument costs no more than 50-100 dollars), it is portable, has a simple structure and form, and it is easy to begin to play. However, it is an instrument where it is difficult to gain expertise, because many of the advanced skills depend on your breath and breathing.

To produce flatter notes, a softer breath is required. Sharper notes can be produced with a harder breath.

Various factors such as the size of the chamber, the size of the whistle window, how well tuned the ocarina is, and the size and smoothness of the air duct all affect the sound and tone of the ocarina. For example, the traditional Italian ocarina usually uses a combination of a very large whistle, an open air duct, and high exhalation air pressure to allow the instrument to reach a maximum volume, but it has a limited range. The difference in the types of ocarina (including shape, number of holes, and key tuning) mean that a player can spend a lifetime mastering each type of ocarina. However, most people can pick it up and play it at a basic level immediately, even if they don't read music.

Ocarinas are made from a variety of materials. The most popular models are made of plastic, porcelain, ceramic, or wood.

We recommend that you avoid ocarinas that are created as artistic pieces, which are richly painted or have complicated shapes, but are not tuned well. Additionally, an ocarina with a unique and artistic shape often can pose problems for the positioning of the fingers, and make it difficult for the holes to be covered properly.

The 6-hole Ocarina can produce a basic scale plus semitone notes, so you can still play more challenging chromatic melodies with it. Our sheet music is based on a 6-hole ocarina tuned in C Major. It covers a pitch range from C5 to E6 and is capable of sharps and flats.

A-Tisket, A-Tasket

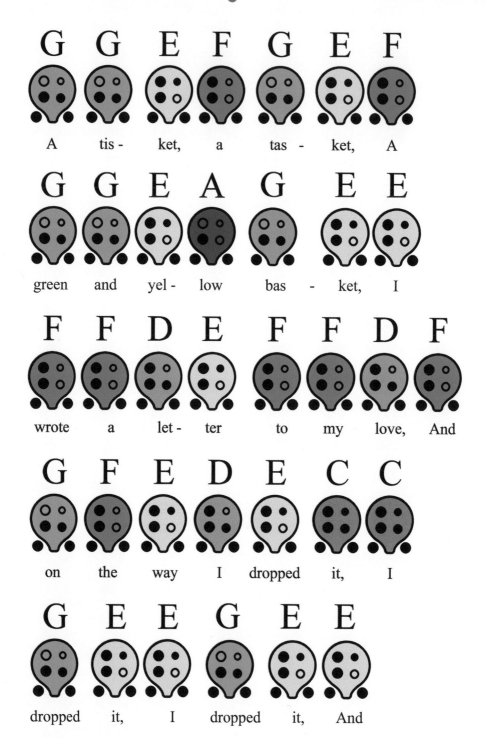

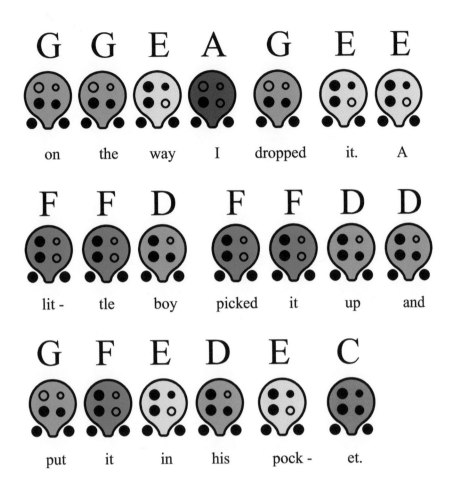

Are You Sleeping?

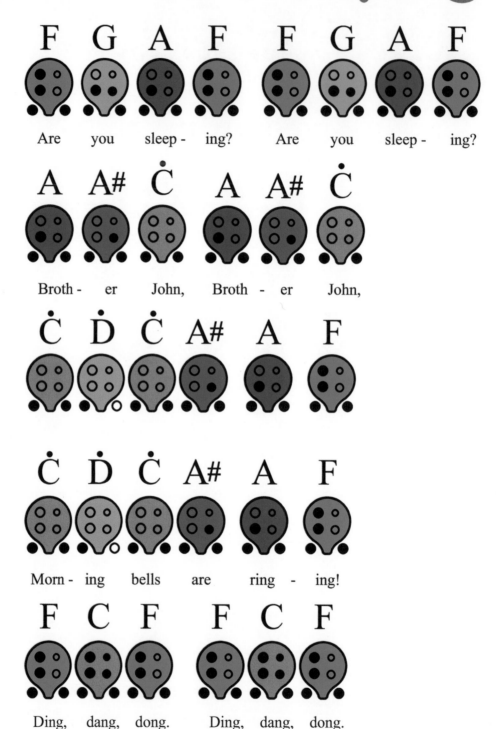

F   G   A   F   F   G   A   F

Are   you   sleep -   ing?   Are   you   sleep -   ing?

A   A#   Ċ   A   A#   Ċ

Broth - er   John,   Broth - er   John,

Ċ   Ḋ   Ċ   A#   A   F

Ċ   Ḋ   Ċ   A#   A   F

Morn - ing   bells   are   ring -   ing!

F   C   F   F   C   F

Ding,   dang,   dong.   Ding,   dang,   dong.

Auld Lang Syne

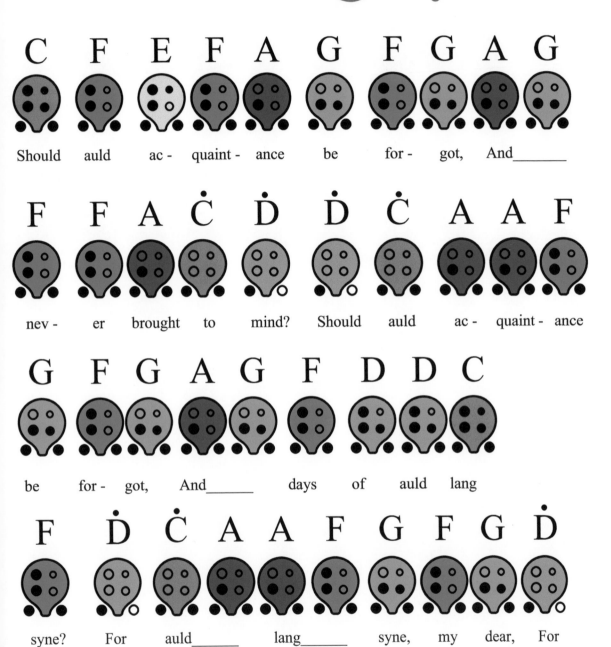

C F E F A G F G A G
Should auld ac - quaint - ance be for - got, And_____

F F A Ċ Ḋ Ḋ Ċ A A F
nev - er brought to mind? Should auld ac - quaint - ance

G F G A G F D D C
be for - got, And_____ days of auld lang

F Ḋ Ċ A A F G F G Ḋ
syne? For auld_____ lang_____ syne, my dear, For

4

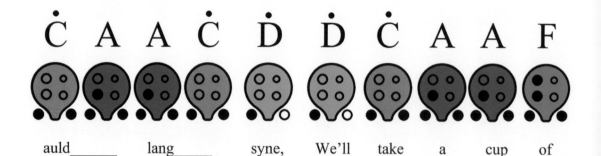

Ċ A A Ċ Ḋ Ḋ Ċ A A F

auld_____ lang____ syne, We'll take a cup of

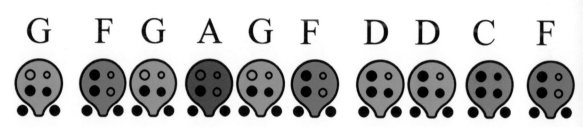

G F G A G F D D C F

kind - ness yet, For_____ auld_____ lang_____ syne.

Aura Lee

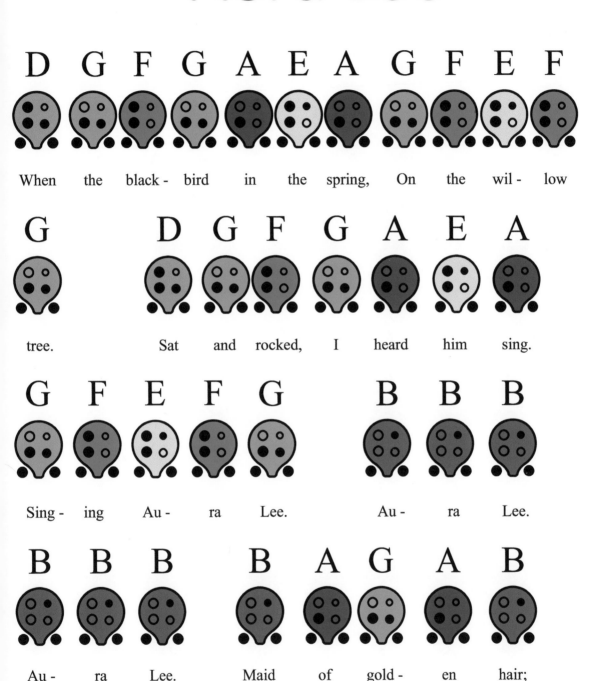

D G F G A E A G F E F

When the black - bird in the spring, On the wil - low

G D G F G A E A

tree. Sat and rocked, I heard him sing.

G F E F G B B B

Sing - ing Au - ra Lee. Au - ra Lee.

B B B B A G A B

Au - ra Lee. Maid of gold - en hair;

Sun - shine came a - long with thee, And

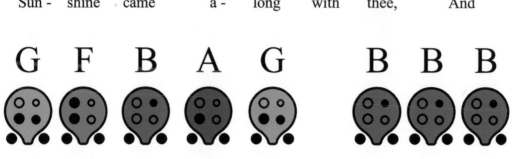

swal - lows in the air. Au - ra Lee_____

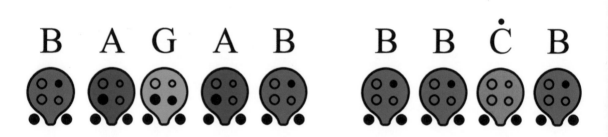

Maid of gold - en hair; Sun - shine came a -

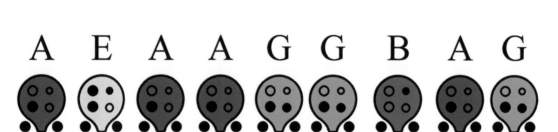

long with thee, And swal - lows in the air.

Au Clair de la Lune

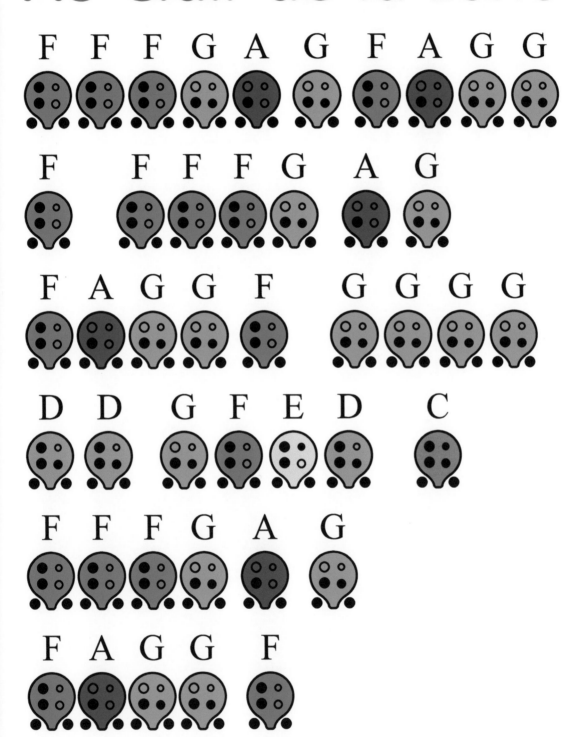

Baa, Baa Black Sheep

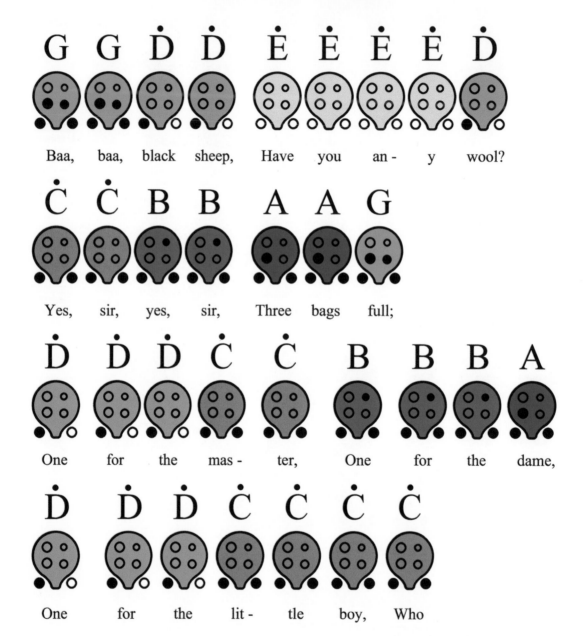

G   G   Ḋ   Ḋ   Ė   Ė   Ė   Ė   Ḋ

Baa,   baa,   black   sheep,   Have   you   an - y   wool?

Ċ   Ċ   B   B   A   A   G

Yes,   sir,   yes,   sir,   Three   bags   full;

Ḋ   Ḋ   Ḋ   Ċ   Ċ   B   B   B   A

One   for   the   mas - ter,   One   for   the   dame,

Ḋ   Ḋ   Ḋ   Ċ   Ċ   Ċ   Ċ

One   for   the   lit - tle   boy,   Who

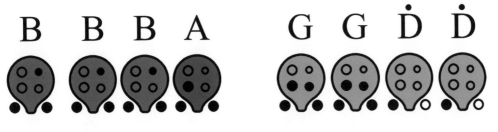

B B B A   G G Ḋ Ḋ

lives down the lane,   Baa, baa, black sheep

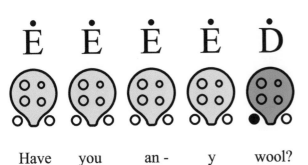

Ė Ė Ė Ė Ḋ

Have you an - y wool?

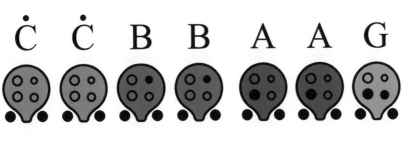

Ċ Ċ B B A A G

Yes, sir, yes, sir, Three bags full.

Bingo

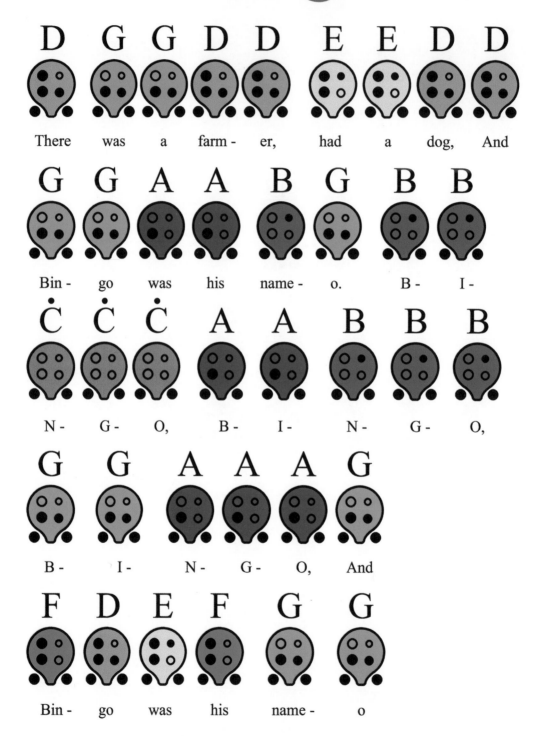

D   G   G   D   D   E   E   D   D

There   was   a   farm -   er,   had   a   dog,   And

G   G   A   A   B   G   B   B

Bin -   go   was   his   name -   o.   B -   I -

Ċ   Ċ   Ċ   A   A   B   B   B

N -   G -   O,   B -   I -   N -   G -   O,

G   G   A   A   A   G

B -   I -   N -   G -   O,   And

F   D   E   F   G   G

Bin -   go   was   his   name -   o

Bye Baby Bunting

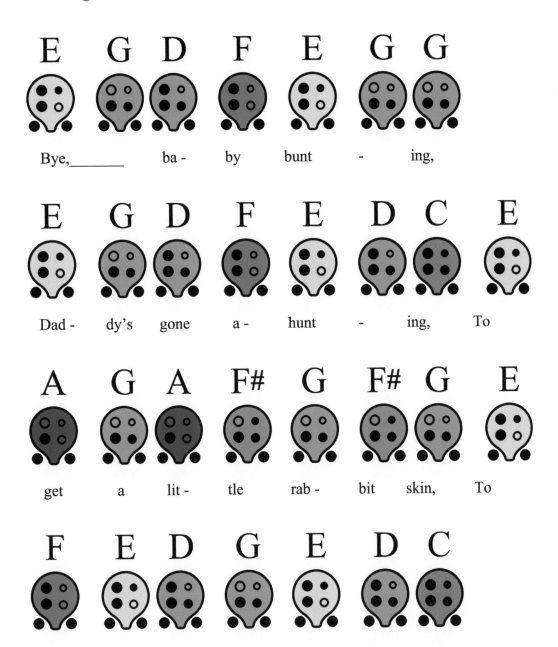

Happy Birthday

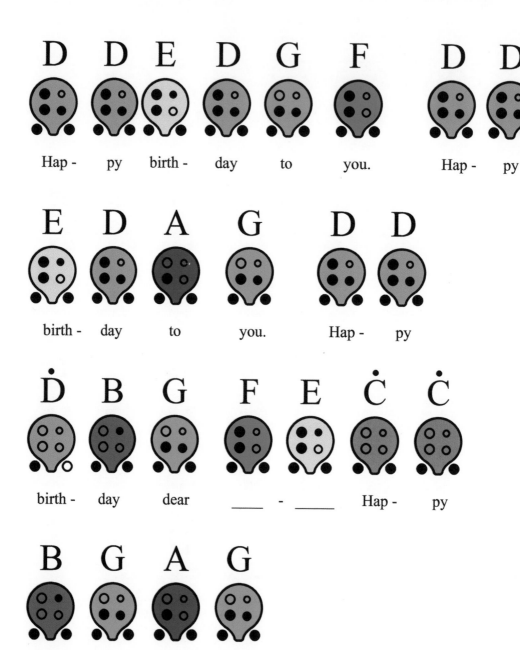

D D E D G F D D
Hap - py birth - day to you. Hap - py

E D A G D D
birth - day to you. Hap - py

Ḋ B G F E Ċ Ċ
birth - day dear ___ - ___ Hap - py

B G A G
birth - day to you.

Here We Go Round the Mulberry Bush

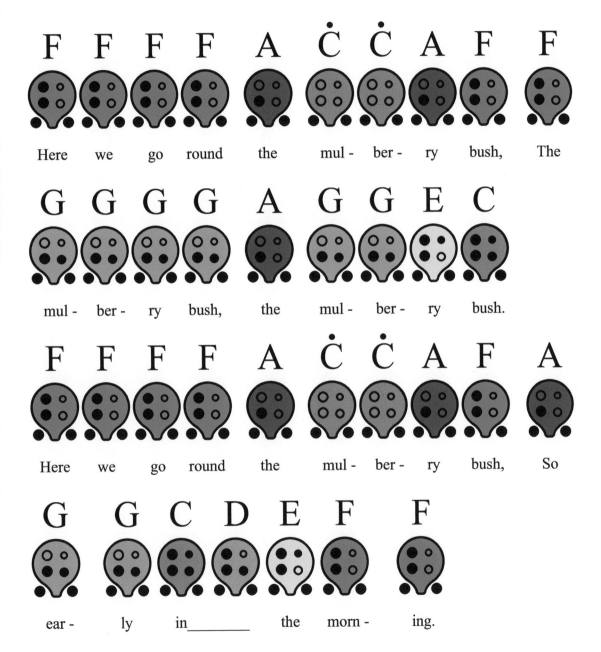

Hey, Diddle Diddle

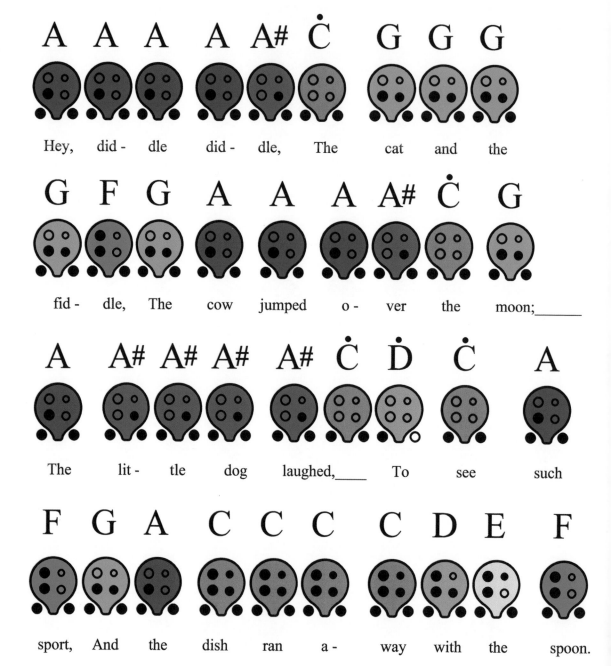

A A A A A# Ċ G G G
Hey, did - dle did - dle, The cat and the

G F G A A A A# Ċ G
fid - dle, The cow jumped o - ver the moon;_____

A A# A# A# A# Ċ Ḋ Ċ A
The lit - tle dog laughed,____ To see such

F G A C C C C D E F
sport, And the dish ran a - way with the spoon.

Hickory Dickory Dock

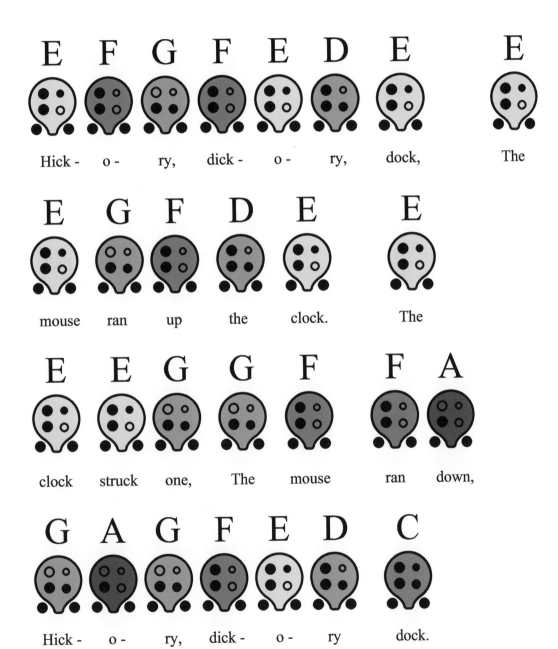

Hot Cross Buns

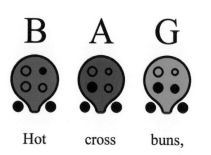

B   A   G   B   A   G

Hot   cross   buns,   Hot   cross   buns,

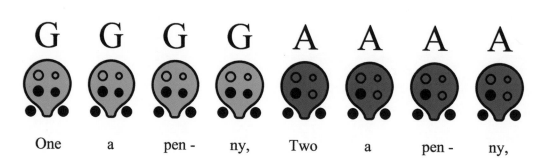

G   G   G   G   A   A   A   A

One   a   pen -   ny,   Two   a   pen -   ny,

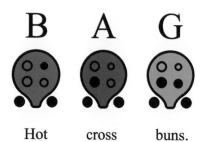

B   A   G

Hot   cross   buns.

Humpty Dumpty

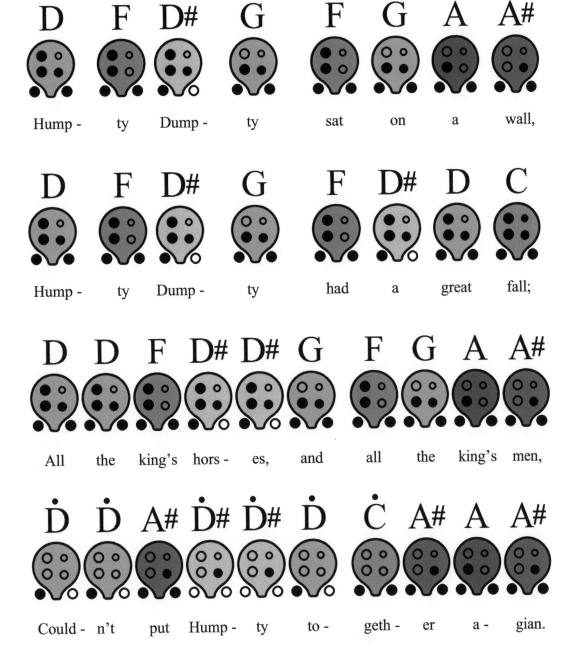

I'm a Little Teapot

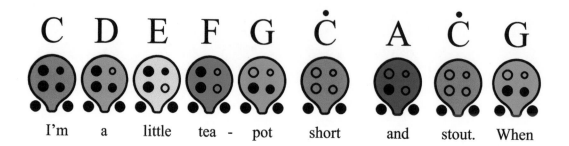

C D E F G Ċ A Ċ G

I'm a little tea - pot short and stout. When

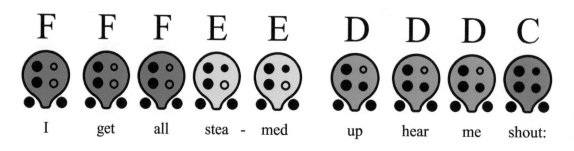

F F F E E D D D C

I get all stea - med up hear me shout:

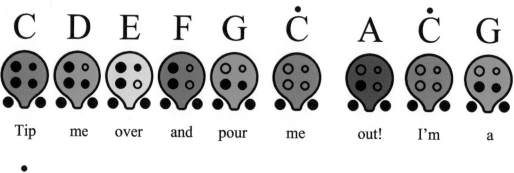

C D E F G Ċ A Ċ G

Tip me over and pour me out! I'm a

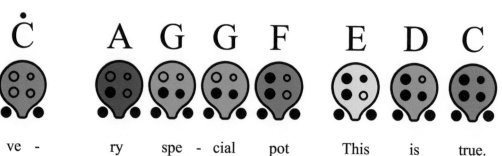

Ċ A G G F E D C

ve - ry spe - cial pot This is true.

If You're Happy and You Know It

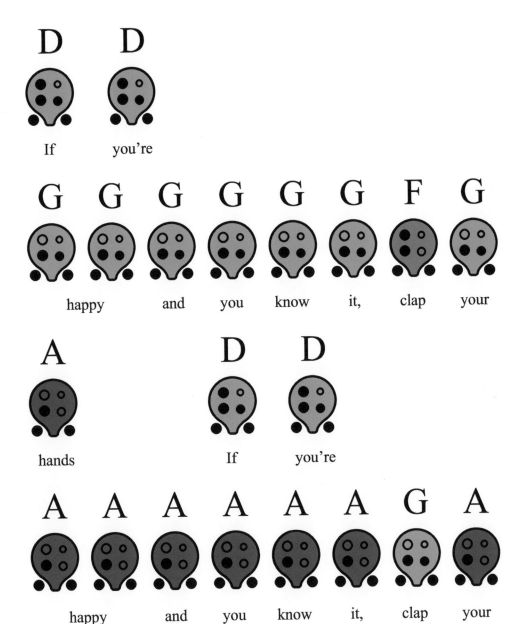

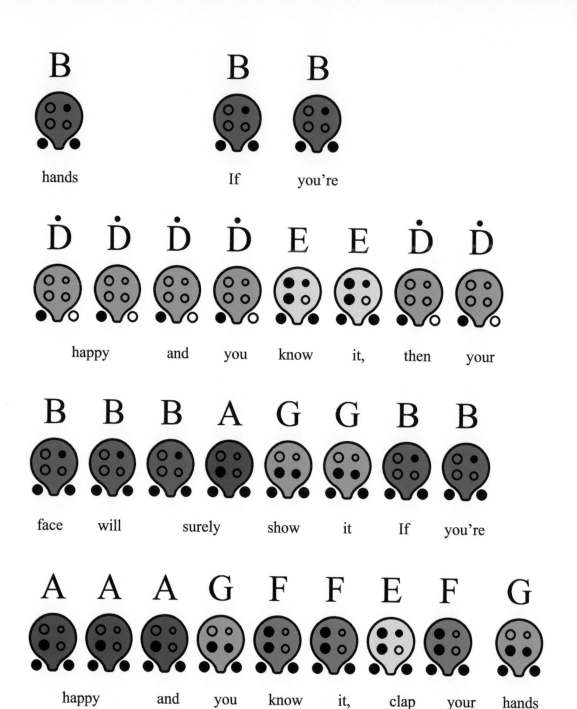

Itsy Bitsy Spider

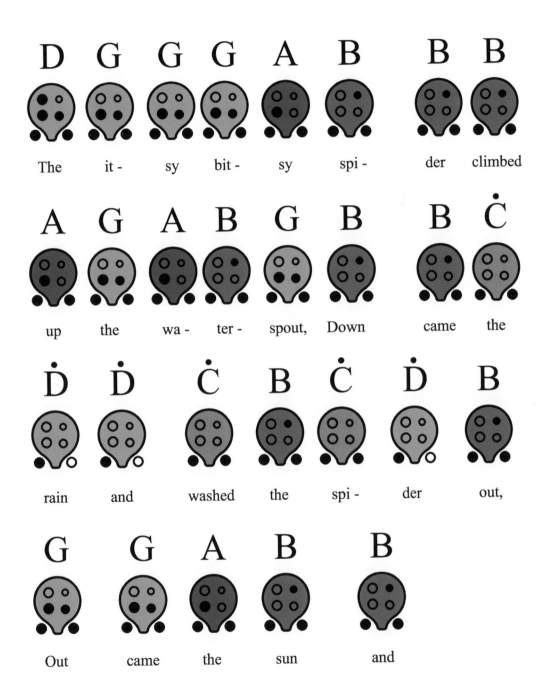

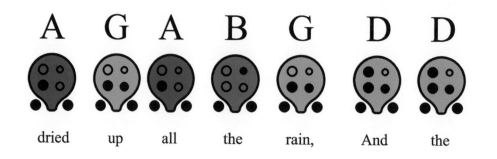

dried   up   all   the   rain,   And   the

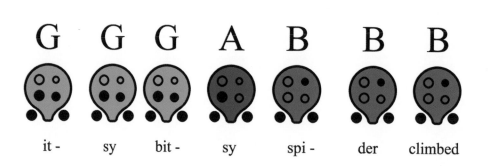

it -   sy   bit -   sy   spi -   der   climbed

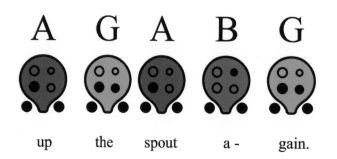

up   the   spout   a -   gain.

Jingle Bells

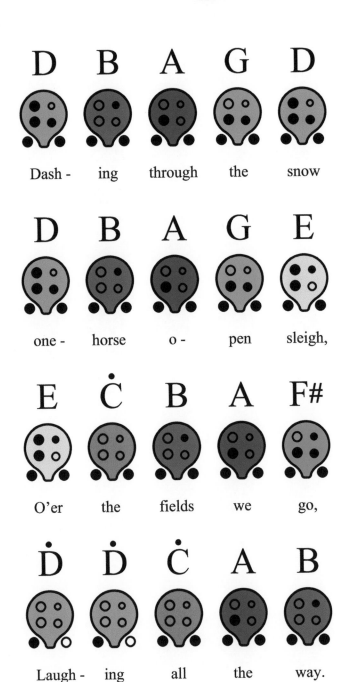

D	B	A	G	D		D	D
Dash -	ing	through	the	snow		In	a

D	B	A	G	E
one -	horse	o -	pen	sleigh,

E	Ċ	B	A	F#
O'er	the	fields	we	go,

Ḋ	Ḋ	Ċ	A	B
Laugh -	ing	all	the	way.

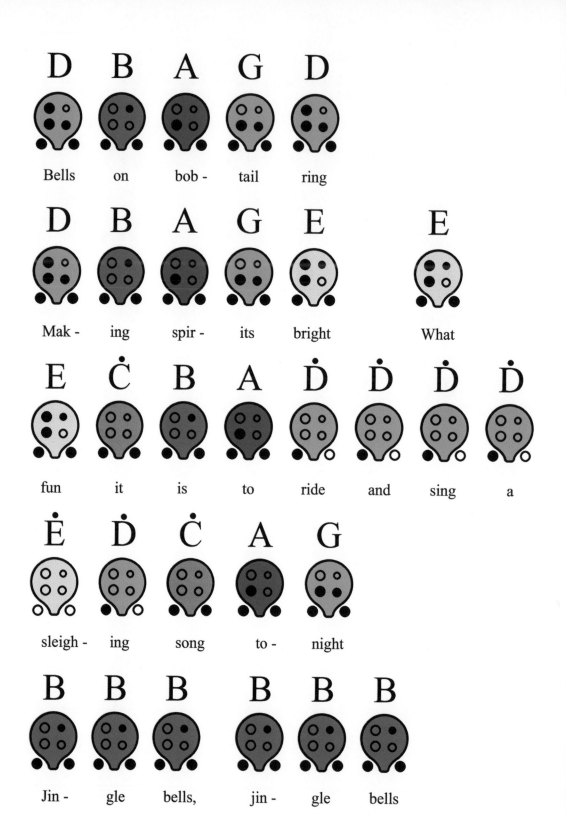

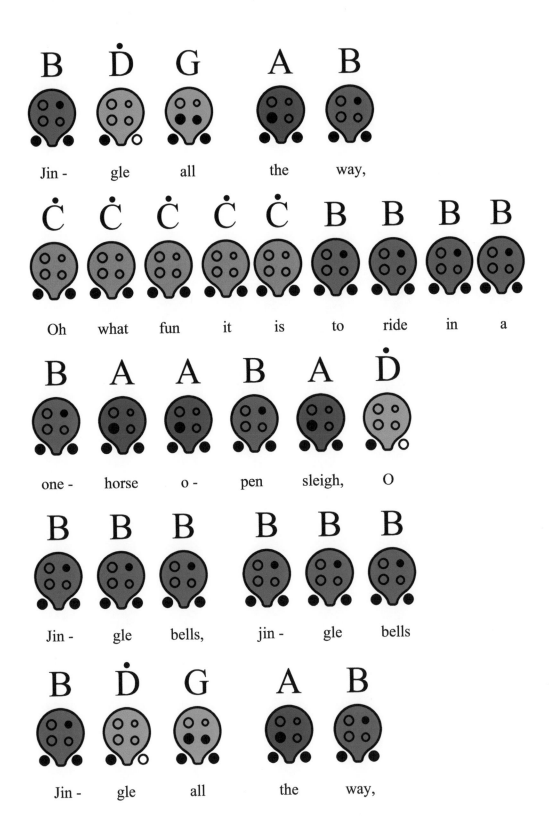

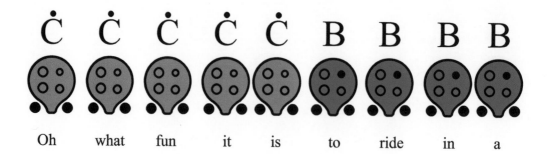

Ċ Ċ Ċ Ċ Ċ B B B B

Oh what fun it is to ride in a

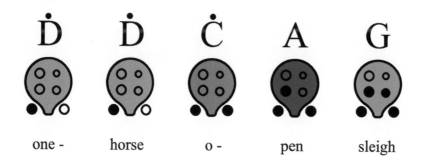

Ḋ Ḋ Ċ A G

one - horse o - pen sleigh

Jolly Old Saint Nicholas

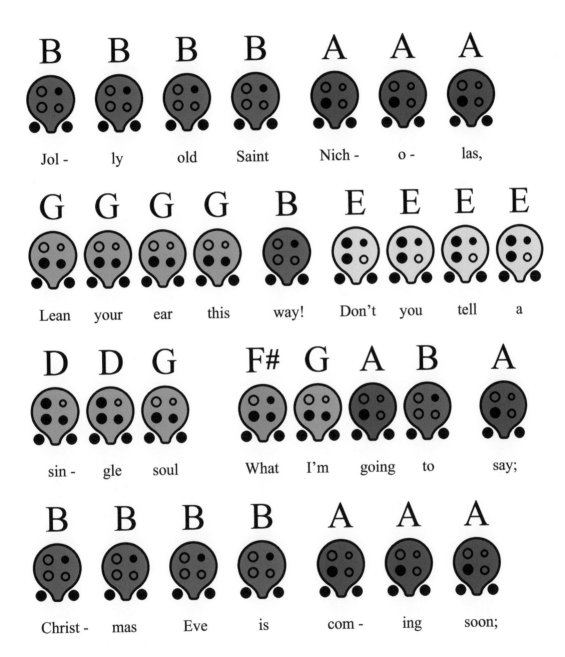

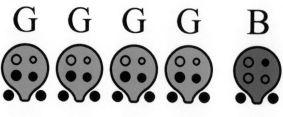

Now you dear old man,

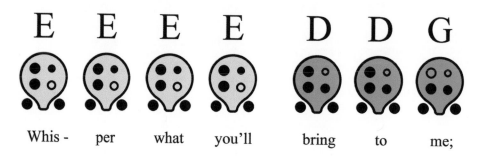

Whis - per what you'll bring to me;

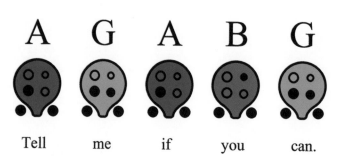

Tell me if you can.

Kumbaya

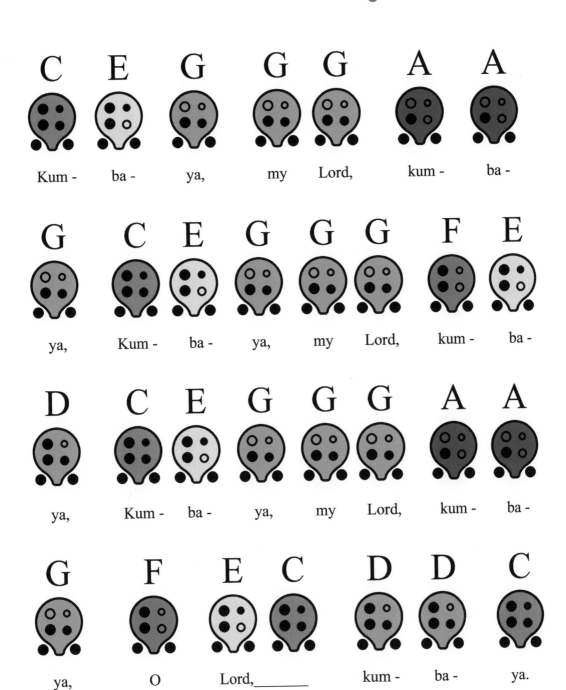

C E G G G A A
Kum - ba - ya, my Lord, kum - ba -

G C E G G G F E
ya, Kum - ba - ya, my Lord, kum - ba -

D C E G G G A A
ya, Kum - ba - ya, my Lord, kum - ba -

G F E C D D C
ya, O Lord,_____ kum - ba - ya.

Lavender's Blue

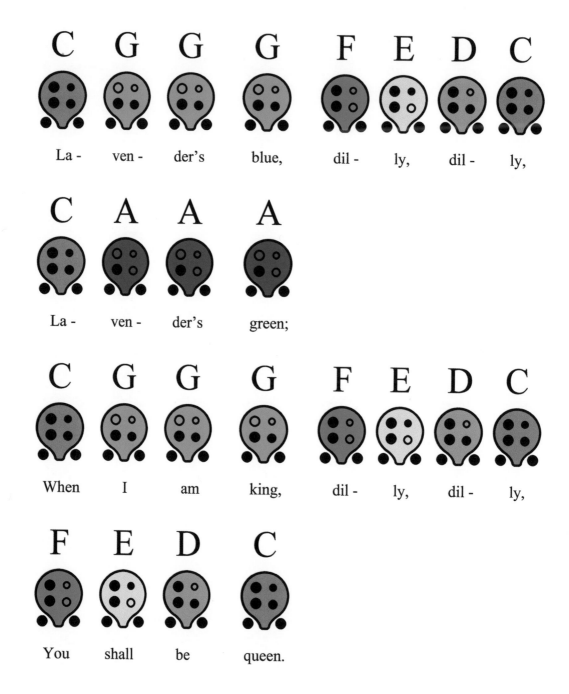

Little Jack Horner

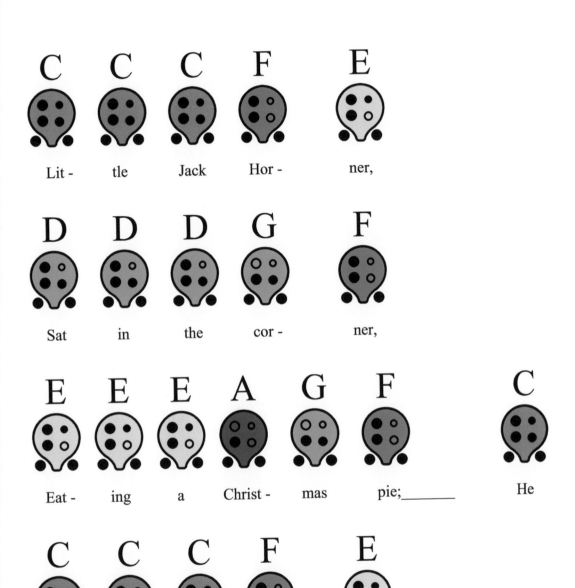

C	C	C	F	E
Lit -	tle	Jack	Hor -	ner,

D	D	D	G	F
Sat	in	the	cor -	ner,

E	E	E	A	G	F	C
Eat -	ing	a	Christ -	mas	pie;_____	He

C	C	C	F	E
put	in	his	thumb,	And

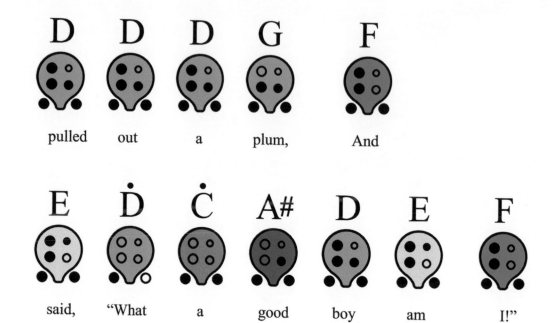

D   D   D   G   F

pulled   out   a   plum,   And

E   Ḋ   Ċ   A#   D   E   F

said,   "What   a   good   boy   am   I!"

London Bridge

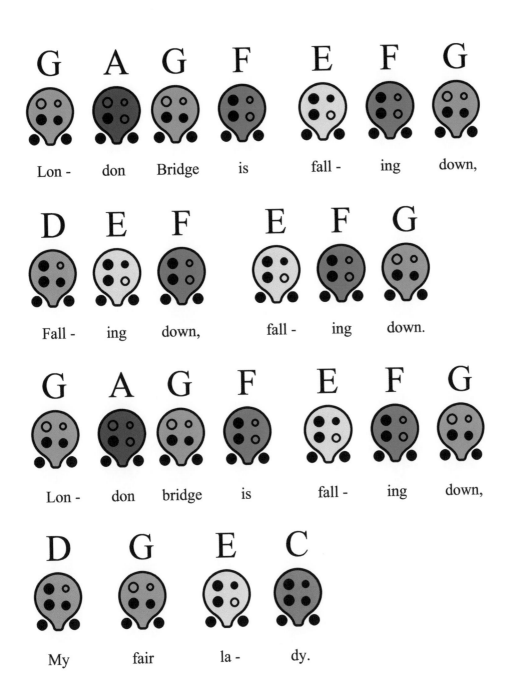

Mary Had a Little Lamb

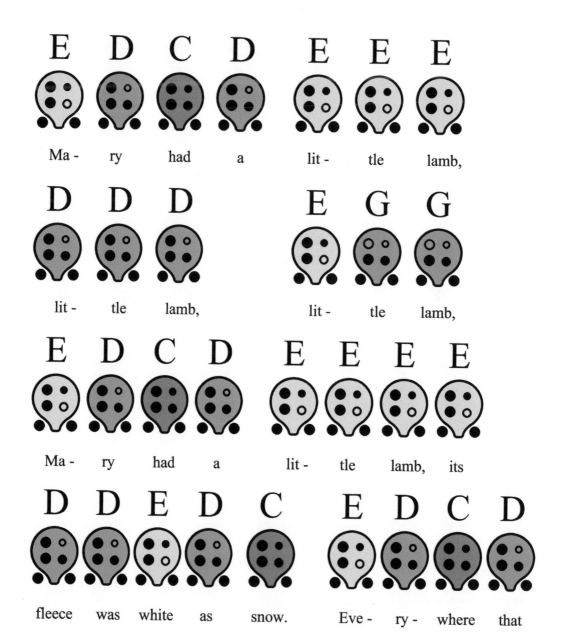

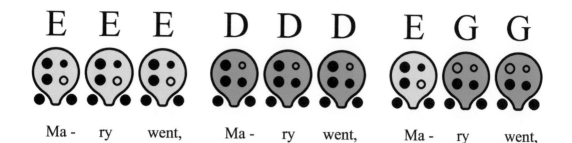

E E E D D D E G G

Ma - ry went, Ma - ry went, Ma - ry went,

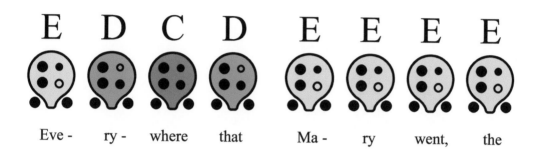

E D C D E E E E

Eve - ry - where that Ma - ry went, the

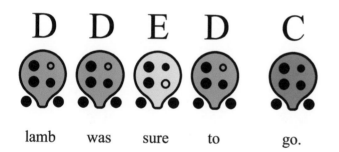

D D E D C

lamb was sure to go.

Misty Mountains

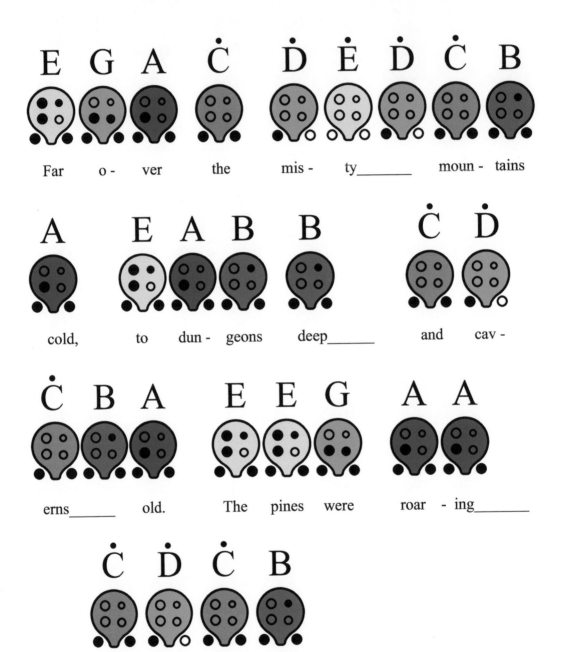

E   G   A   Ċ   Ḋ   Ė   Ḋ   Ċ   B

Far   o -   ver   the   mis -   ty_____   moun - tains

A   E   A   B   B   Ċ   Ḋ

cold,   to   dun - geons   deep_____   and   cav -

Ċ   B   A   E   E   G   A   A

erns_____   old.   The   pines   were   roar   - ing_____

Ċ   Ḋ   Ċ   B

____   o   -   n

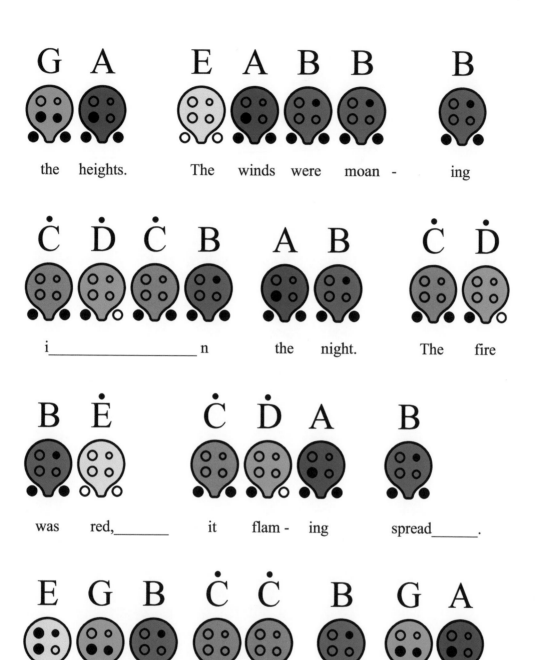

G A   E A B B   B
the heights.   The winds were moan - ing

Ċ Ḋ Ċ B   A B   Ċ Ḋ
i_____n   the night.   The fire

B Ė   Ċ Ḋ A   B
was red,_____   it flam - ing   spread_____.

E G B Ċ Ċ   B   G A
The trees like tor - ches,   blazed   with light._____

My Bonny Lies Over the Ocean

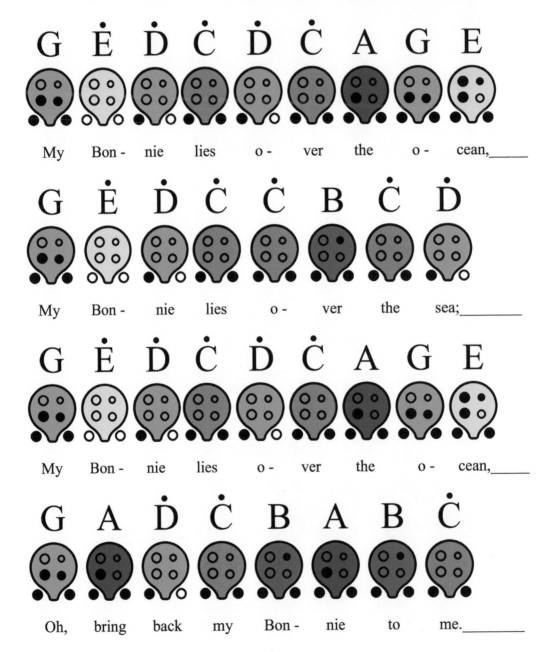

G Ė D Ċ D Ċ A G E
My Bon - nie lies o - ver the o - cean,_____

G Ė D Ċ Ċ B Ċ D
My Bon - nie lies o - ver the sea;_____

G Ė D Ċ D Ċ A G E
My Bon - nie lies o - ver the o - cean,_____

G A D Ċ B A B Ċ
Oh, bring back my Bon - nie to me._____

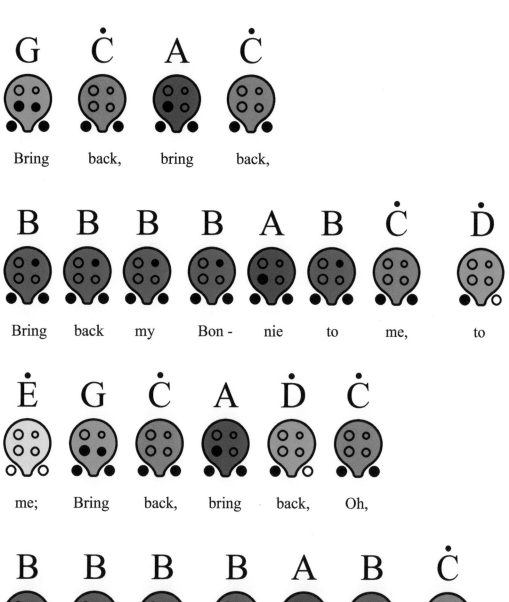
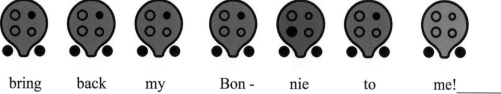

O, Christmas Tree (O, Tannenbaum)

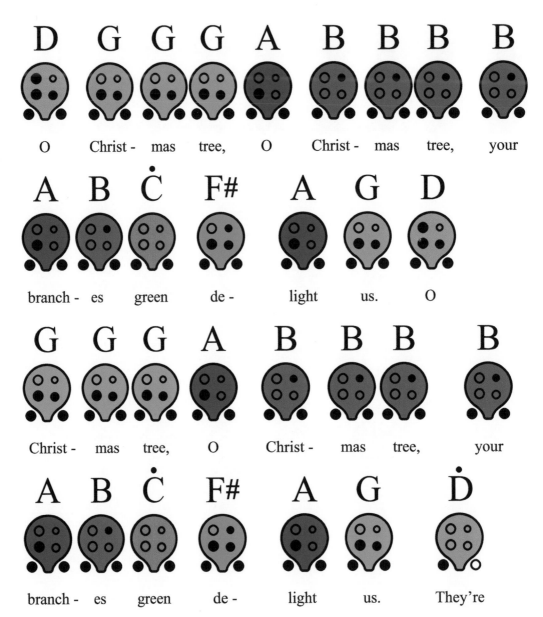

D G G G A B B B B
O   Christ - mas   tree,   O   Christ - mas   tree,   your

A B Ċ F# A G D
branch - es   green   de -   light   us.   O

G G G A B B B B
Christ - mas   tree,   O   Christ -   mas   tree,   your

A B Ċ F# A G Ḋ
branch - es   green   de -   light   us.   They're

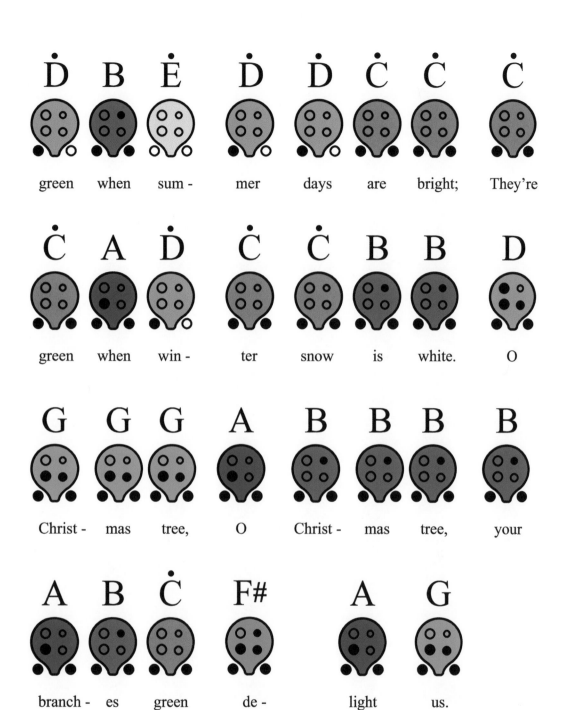

Oh My Darling, Clementine

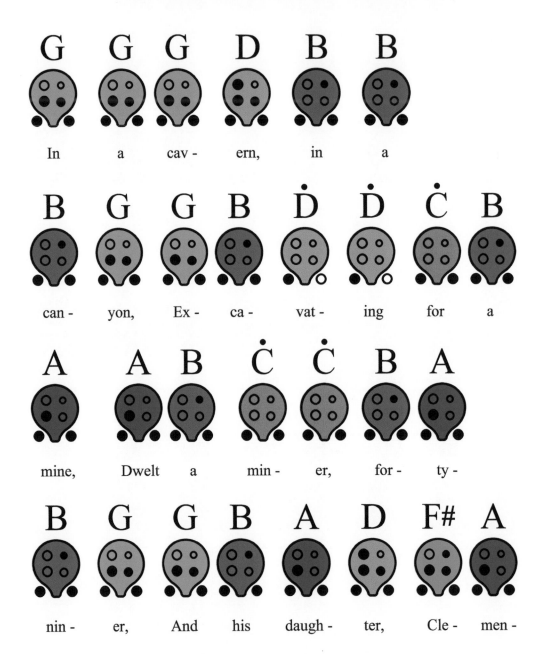

G   G   G   D   B   B

In   a   cav -   ern,   in   a

B   G   G   B   Ḋ   Ḋ   Ċ   B

can -   yon,   Ex -   ca -   vat -   ing   for   a

A   A   B   Ċ   Ċ   B   A

mine,   Dwelt   a   min -   er,   for -   ty -

B   G   G   B   A   D   F#   A

nin -   er,   And   his   daugh -   ter,   Cle -   men -

43

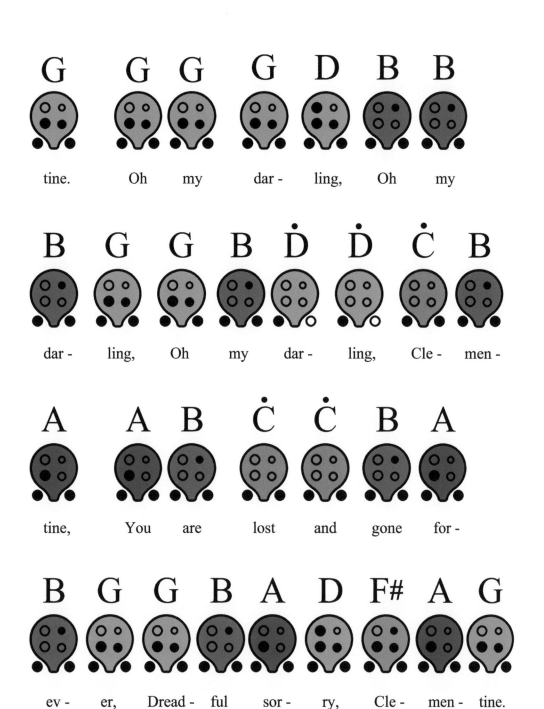

Old MacDonald Had a Farm

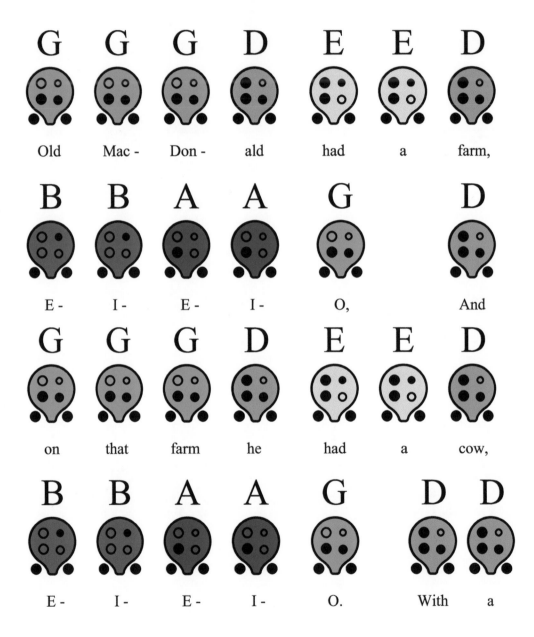

G	G	G	D	E	E	D
Old	Mac -	Don -	ald	had	a	farm,

B	B	A	A	G		D
E -	I -	E -	I -	O,		And

G	G	G	D	E	E	D
on	that	farm	he	had	a	cow,

B	B	A	A	G	D	D
E -	I -	E -	I -	O.	With	a

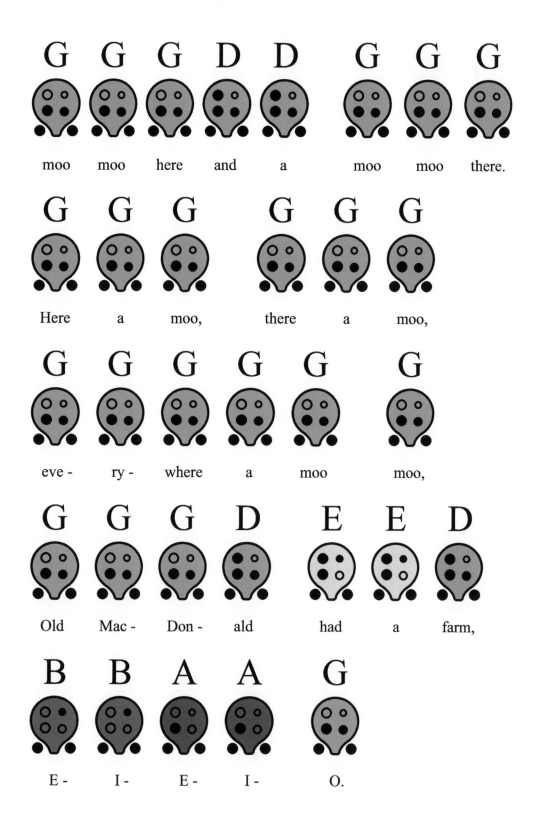

Rain, Rain, Go Away

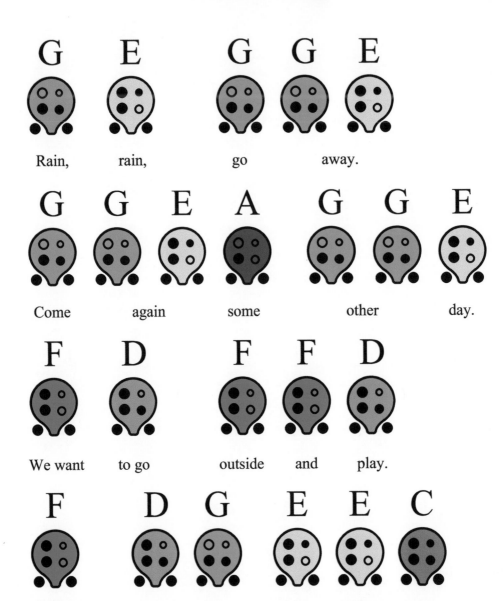

Pop! Goes the Weasel

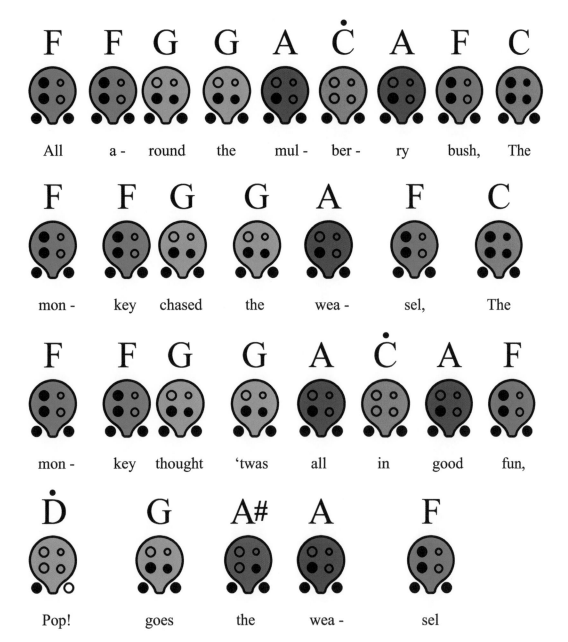

Ring Around the Rosie

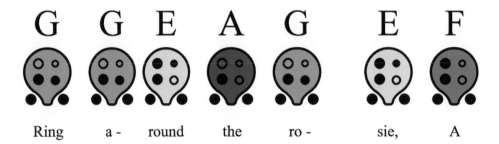

G   G   E   A   G   E   F

Ring   a -   round   the   ro -   sie,   A

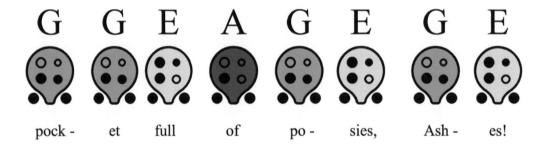

G   G   E   A   G   E   G   E

pock -   et   full   of   po -   sies,   Ash -   es!

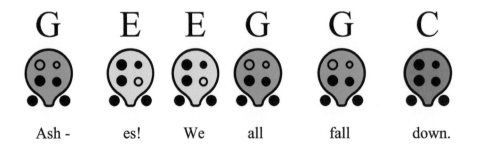

G   E   E   G   G   C

Ash -   es!   We   all   fall   down.

Row Row Row Your Boat

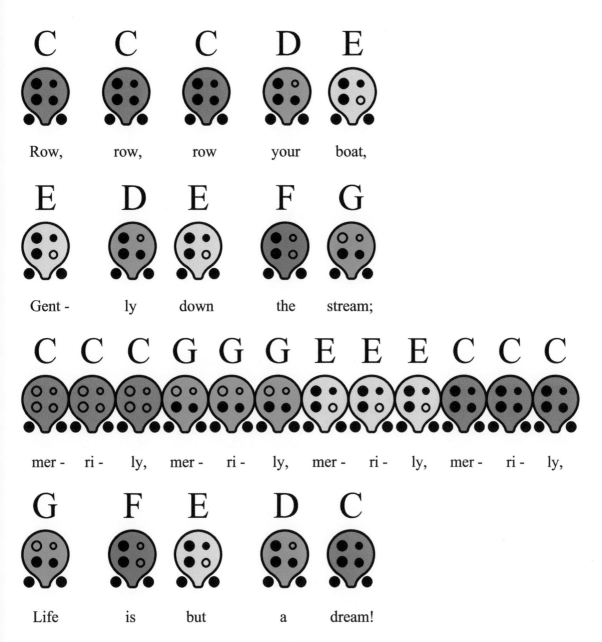

The Bear Went Over the Mountain

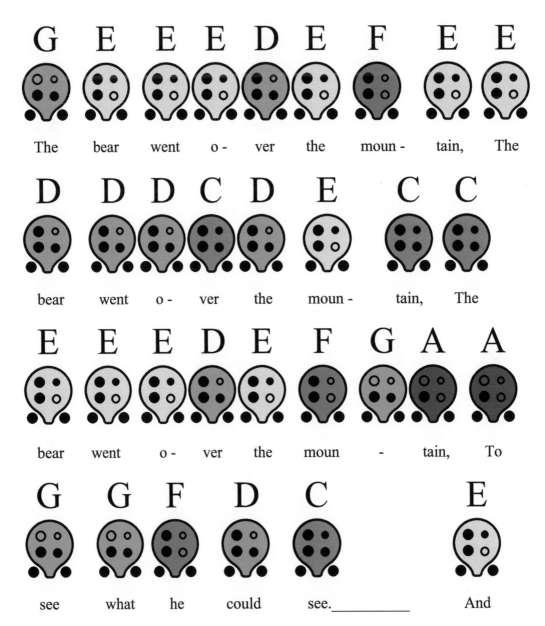

G E E E D E F E E

The bear went o - ver the moun - tain, The

D D D C D E C C

bear went o - ver the moun - tain, The

E E E D E F G A A

bear went o - ver the moun - tain, To

G G F D C E

see what he could see._____ And

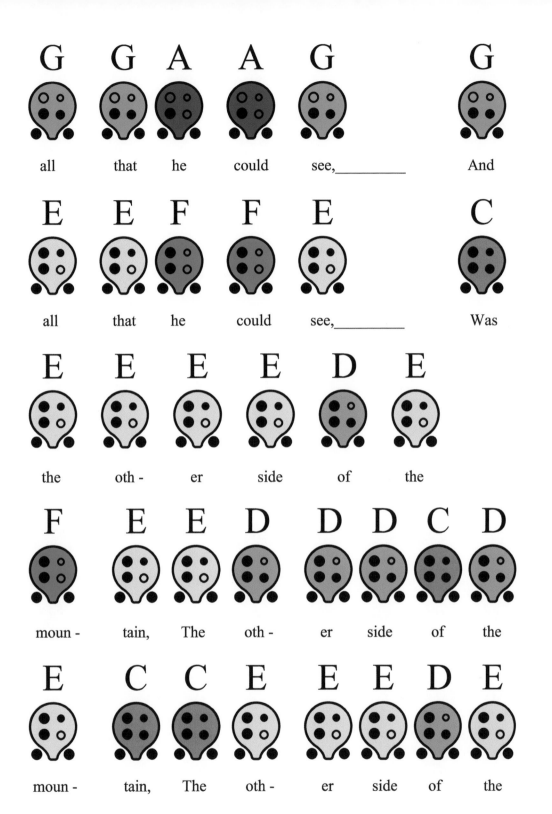

moun   -   tain,   Was

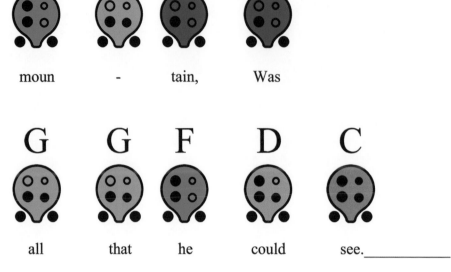

all   that   he   could   see._____

The First Noel

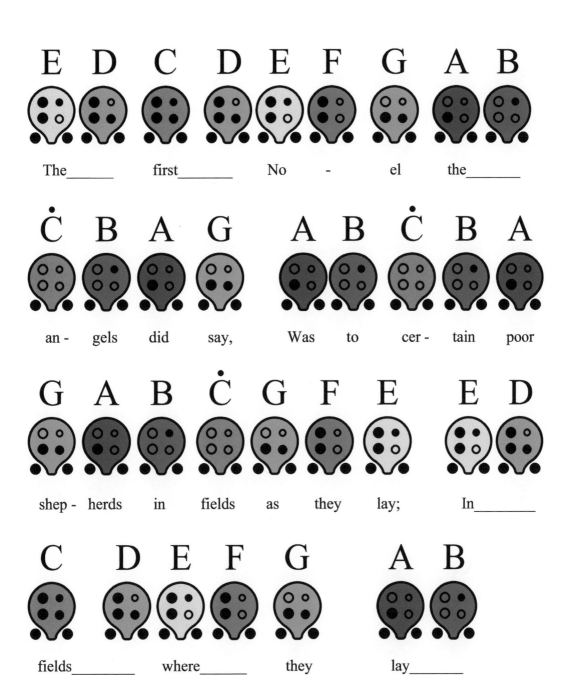

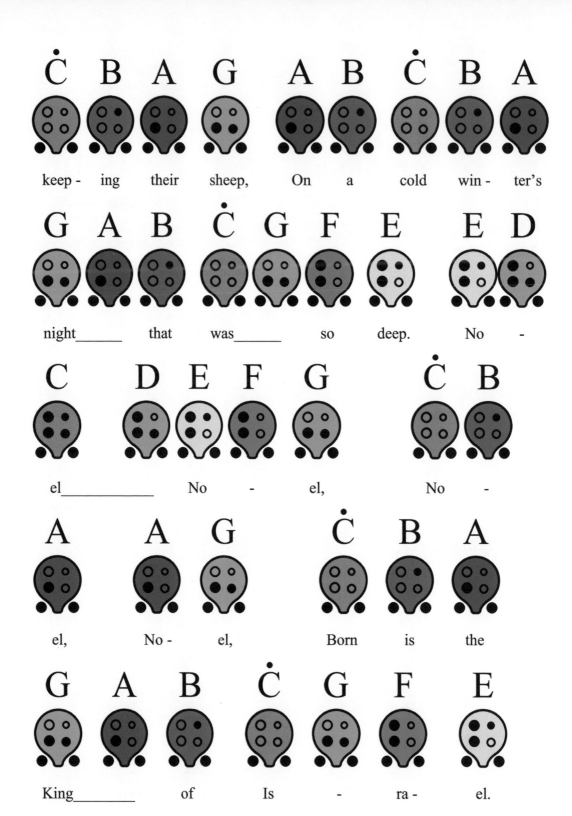

The Muffin Man

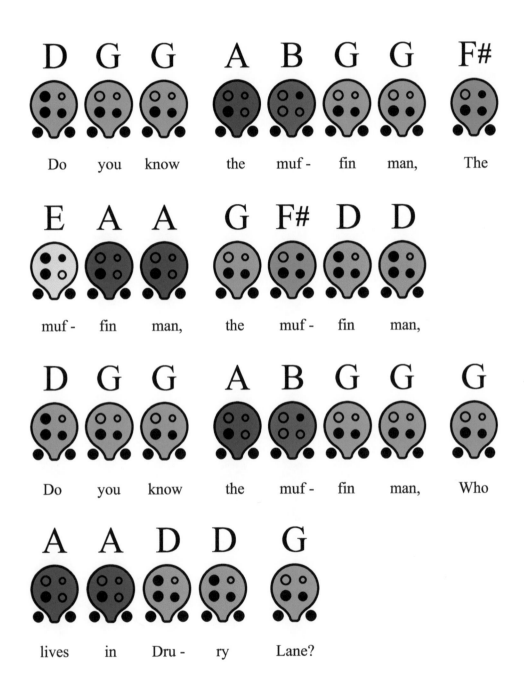

This Old Man

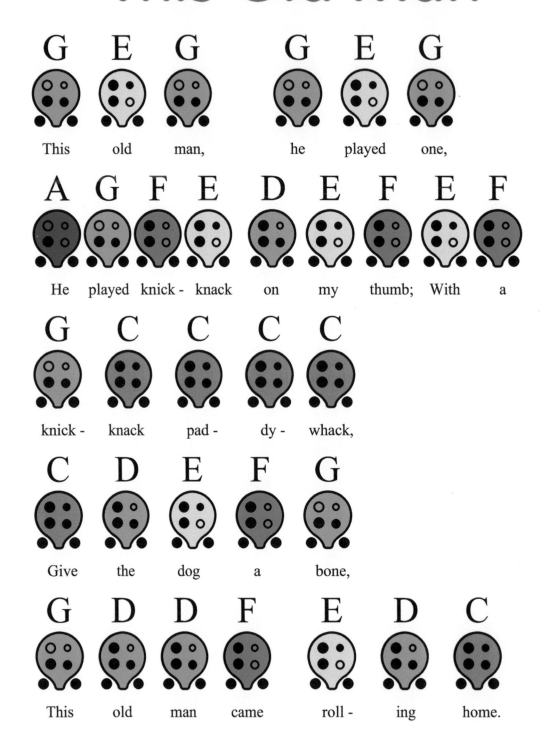

The Wheels on the Bus

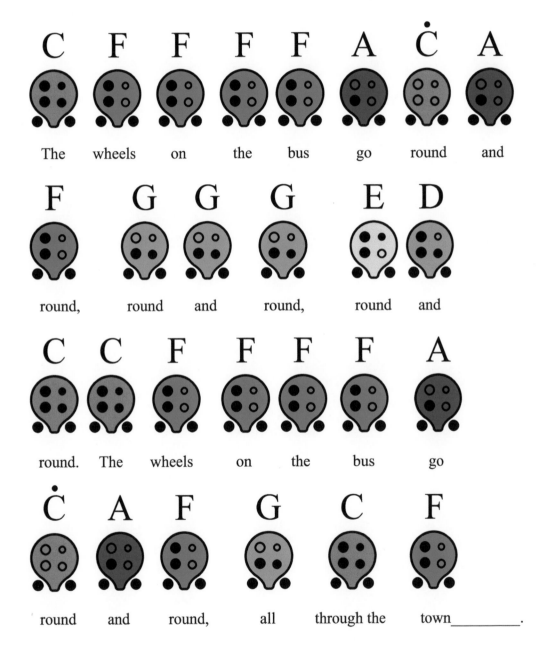

Ten Little Fingers

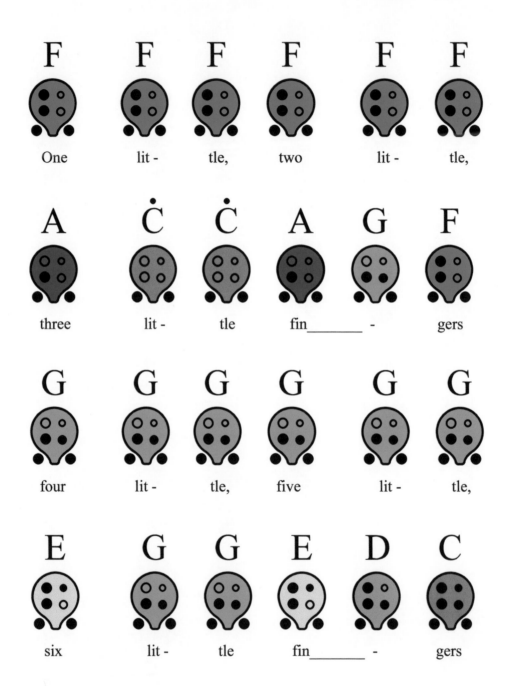

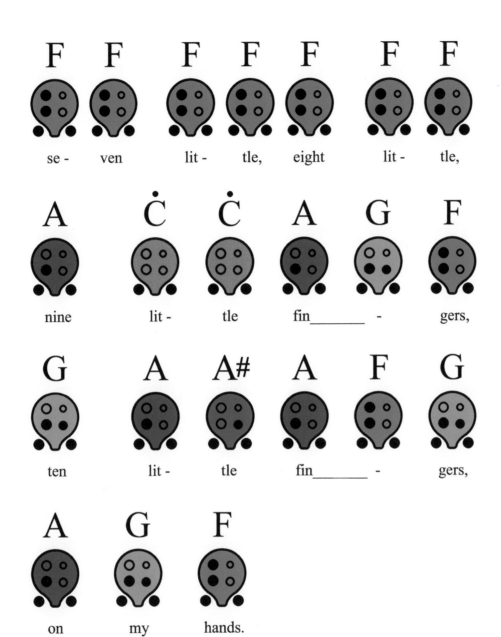

Twinkle, Twinkle Little Star

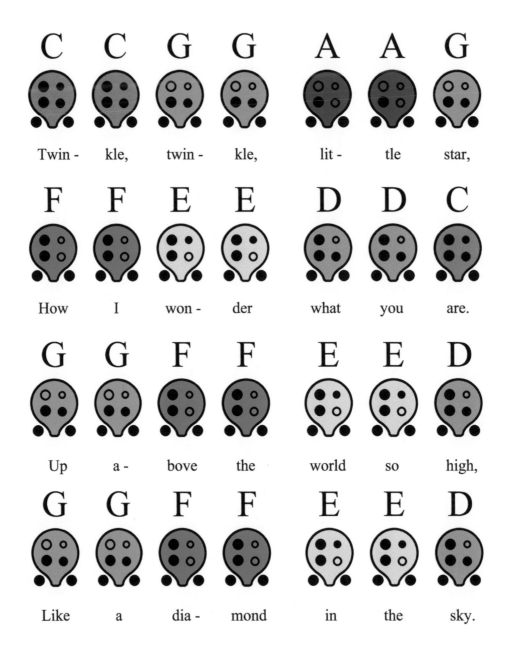

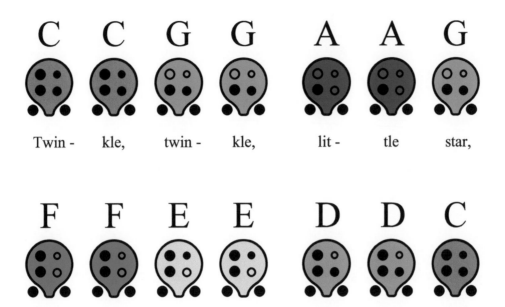

We Wish You a Merry Christmas

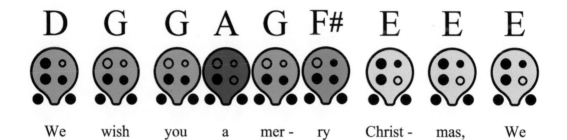

D   G   G   A   G   F#   E   E   E

We   wish   you   a   mer -   ry   Christ -   mas,   We

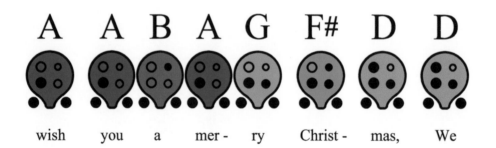

A   A   B   A   G   F#   D   D

wish   you   a   mer -   ry   Christ -   mas,   We

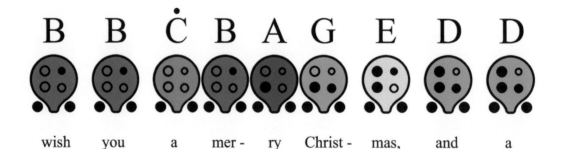

B   B   Ċ   B   A   G   E   D   D

wish   you   a   mer -   ry   Christ -   mas,   and   a

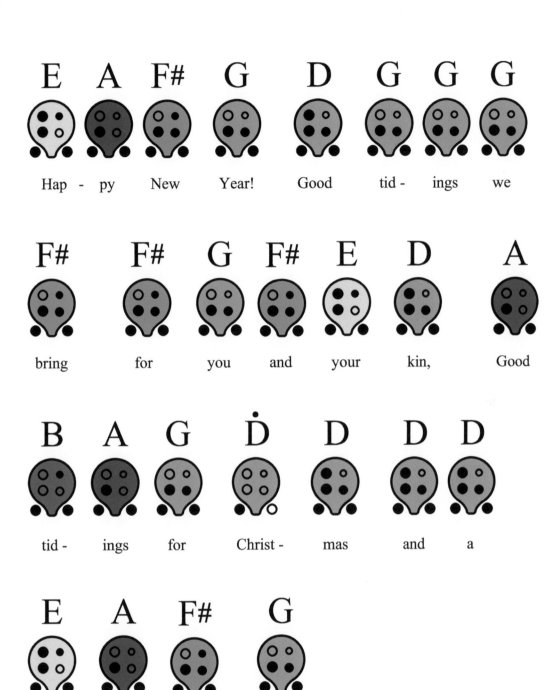

When the Saints Go Marching In!

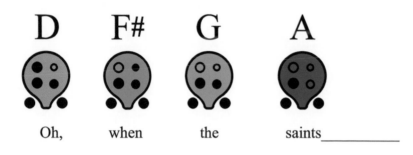

D   F#   G   A

Oh,   when   the   saints_____

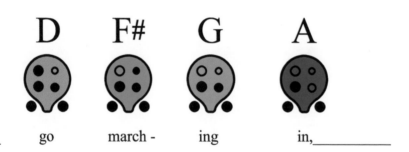

D   F#   G   A

_____   go   march -   ing   in,_____

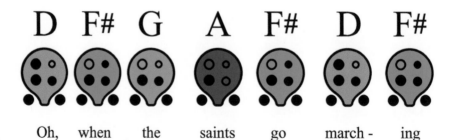

D   F#   G   A   F#   D   F#

_____   Oh,   when   the   saints   go   march -   ing

in,_____   Oh   Lord,   I   want   to

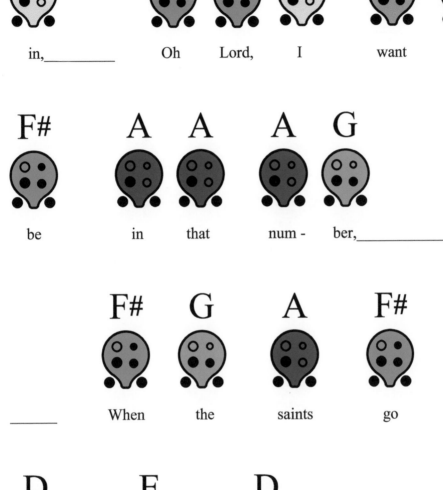

be   in   that   num -   ber,_____

_____   When   the   saints   go

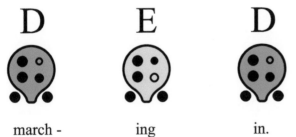

march -   ing   in.

What Shall We Do With the Drunken Sailor

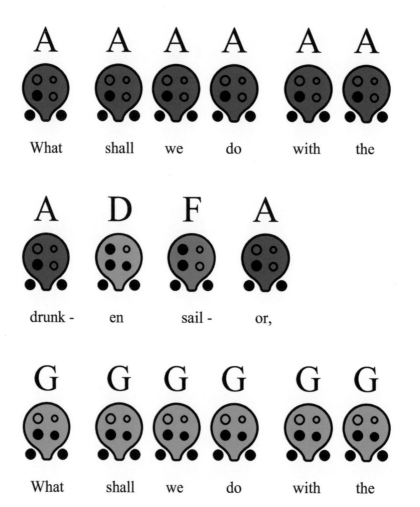

A   A   A   A   A   A

What   shall   we   do   with   the

A   D   F   A

drunk -   en   sail -   or,

G   G   G   G   G   G

What   shall   we   do   with   the

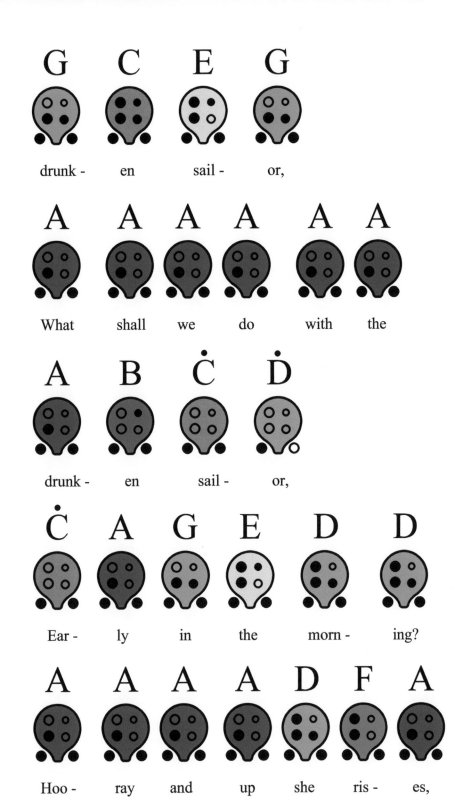

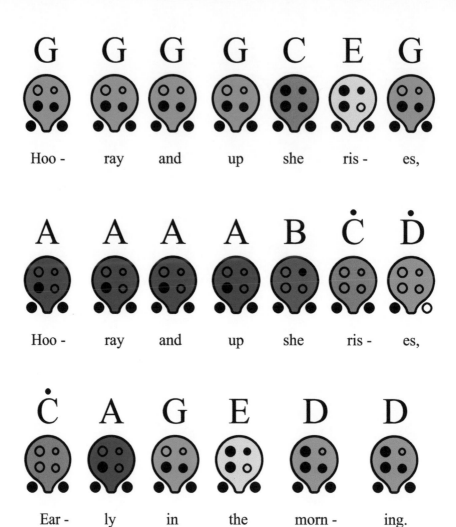

G G G G C E G
Hoo - ray and up she ris - es,

A A A A B Ċ Ḋ
Hoo - ray and up she ris - es,

Ċ A G E D D
Ear - ly in the morn - ing.

99 Bottles of Beer

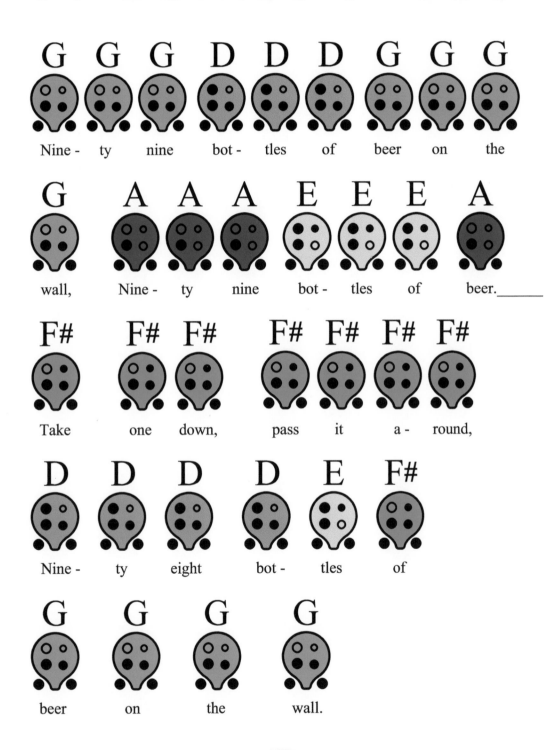

Printed in Great Britain
by Amazon

19662521R00042